D0572929

HOW TO DRAW
BIG CATS

Grrrr!

Carolyn Franklin

PowerKiDS press

New York

Published in 2009 by The Rosen Publishing Group, Inc.
29 East 21st Street, New York, NY 10010

Editor: Rob Walker
U.S. Editor: Kara Murray

Library of Congress Cataloging-in-Publication Data

Franklin, Carolyn, 1956–
  Big cats / Carolyn Franklin. — 1st ed.
     p. cm. — (How to draw)
  Includes index.
   ISBN 978-1-4358-2516-1 (library binding)
  ISBN 978-1-4358-2645-8 (pb binding)
  ISBN 978-1-4358-2657-1 (6-pack)
  1. Felidae in art—Juvenile literature. 2. Drawing—
Technique—Juvenile literature. I. Title.
   NC783.8.F45F73 2009
   743.6'9755—dc22

                                            2008001134

Manufactured in China

Contents

4   Making a Start

6   Drawing Tools

8   Anatomy

10   Using Photographs

12   Style and Medium

14   Tiger

16   Lion

18   Panther

20   Tiger's Head

22   Leopard

24   Lynx

26   Cheetah

28   Lion Cubs

30   Puma

32   Glossary, Index, and Web Sites

Making a Start

Drawing is lots of fun and very exciting! You don't need expensive equipment. Use whatever materials are handy: scraps of paper, cardboard packaging, or old greeting cards. Try using pencils, crayons, pens, or charcoal. You can draw with paint, too. Just use a brush, a stick, or even your finger.

Grrrr!

Start by doodling and experimenting with shapes and patterns.

Fingerprint and black felt-tip pen

Soft pencil

Pencil shading

Felt-tip pen dots

Fingerprint and felt-tip pen

Textures

Wet a sheet of paper and draw on it with a felt-tip pen. See how the ink runs and the lines soften. Experiment by drawing on papers with different textures. Try sketching in white pastel on black or gray paper (see page 6).

Sketching

Carry a sketch pad with you at all times. Your drawing will get better the more you draw and sketch.

A sketch pad is your working record of ideas and ways of drawing.

Black felt-tip pen with clear water wash and hard pencil

Ball-point pen and hard pencil

Ball-point pen

Soft pencil

Gray felt-tip pen with clear water wash and hard pencil

Gray felt-tip pen and pencil shading

Pencil fingerprint and ink wash

5

Drawing Tools

Here are just a few of the many tools that you can use for drawing. Let your imagination go and have fun experimenting with all the different marks you can make.

Pencil

Watercolor pencil

Charcoal pencil

Charcoal stick

Pastels

Finger painting

Black, gray, and white pastel on gray sugar paper

Different grades of pencil make different marks, from fine, gray lines to soft, black ones. Pencils are graded from #1 (the softest) to #4 (the hardest).

Watercolor pencils come in many different colors and make a line similar to a #2 pencil. Paint over your finished drawing with clean water and the lines will soften and run.

It is less messy and easier to achieve a fine line with a **charcoal pencil** than a **charcoal stick**. Create soft tones by smudging lines with your finger. Spray with fixative to prevent further smudging.

Pastels are brittle sticks of powdered color. They blend and smudge easily and are ideal for quick sketches. Pastel drawings work well on textured, colored paper. Spray your drawing with fixative when your drawing is finished.

Experiment with finger painting. Your fingerprints make exciting patterns and textures. Use your fingers to smudge soft pencil, charcoal, and pastel lines.

Ball-point pens are very useful for sketching and making notes. Make different tones by building up layers of shading.

A **mapping pen** has to be dipped into bottled ink to fill the nib. Different nib shapes make different marks. Try putting a diluted ink wash over parts of the finished drawing.

Draftsman's pens and specialty art pens can produce extremely fine lines and are ideal for creating fur markings. A variety of pen nibs are available, which produce different widths of line.

Felt-tip pens are ideal for quick sketches. If the ink is not waterproof, try drawing on wet paper and see the effect.

Broad-nibbed marker pens make interesting lines and are good for large, bold sketches. Try using a black pen for the main sketch and a gray one to block in areas of shadow.

Paintbrushes are shaped differently to make different marks. Japanese brushes are soft and produce beautiful flowing lines. Large sable brushes are good for painting a wash over a line drawing. Fine brushes are good for drawing the delicate lines of whiskers and fur.

Ball-point pen

Mapping pen

Draftsman's pen

Felt-tip pen

Marker pen

Paintbrush

7

Anatomy

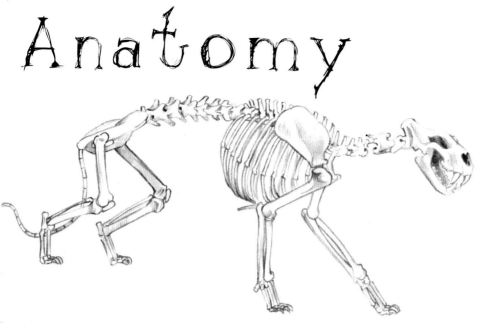

Skeleton of a leopard

Musculature of a leopard

Study the skeleton. See how the leopard's front and back legs bend. Look at the position of the muscles and see how they wrap around the skeleton.

Movement and muscles

Watch the movement of a domestic cat to see how it walks, runs, and lies down. Compare the drawing of the leopard's skeleton to the drawing on this page. Understanding how an animal's skeleton moves and where its major muscles lie will help make your drawings more realistic and lively.

Look and learn

Some cats have a longer, leaner look than others. Study each cat before you start to draw.

Using Photographs

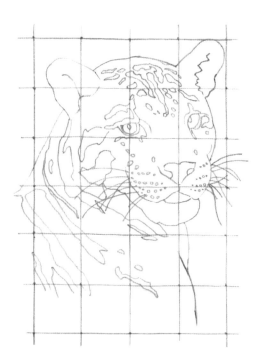

It is always best to draw something you can actually see. However, you can still produce a lifelike drawing by using a photograph as a reference.

Drawing from photographs

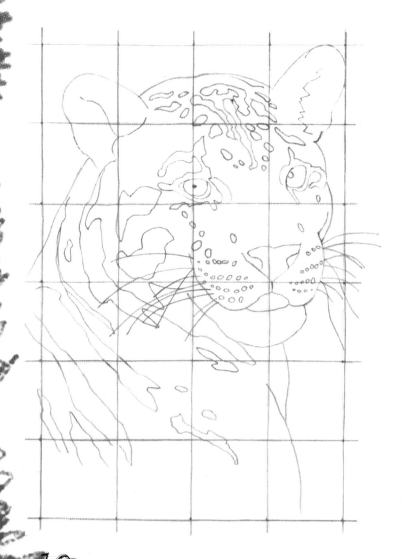

Grids

Make a tracing of the photograph and draw a grid over it (above).

Tracing

Lightly draw another grid in the same proportions on your drawing paper. You can now transfer the shapes from your tracing to your drawing paper using these grids as a guide (left). This method is called squaring up.

Drawing in three dimensions

A drawing of a photograph can look too flat.
Make your drawing look more three-dimensional
by checking how light falls on the tiger's head
and then shade in the dark areas.

Areas of shade

Tones and focal points

Draw in the midtone gray fur. Leave areas
of the paper untouched for white fur. Pay
special attention when drawing the cat's
eyes, as they are the focal point of the
drawing. Draw in the dark stripes and use a
fine paintbrush with white paint to draw
the whiskers.

Style and Medium

You can transform a drawing simply by changing the medium you use.

Try drawing the same image but using different techniques and on various types and sizes of paper.

This tiger cub was sketched in charcoal with a light wash of black watercolor.

This snow leopard was drawn with a felt-tip pen. Then a light wash of water was painted over parts of it.

Black and white pastels were used on gray textured paper to draw this leopard.

This tiger was first drawn in pencil. Masking fluid was painted over some areas of the picture and then a watercolor wash was added. When dry, the masking fluid was rubbed off using a soft eraser. These areas have been kept white.

Tiger

The tiger is the largest and the heaviest of the cat family. It usually hunts alone, charging after its prey from about 65 feet (20 m) away. A tiger kills its victim by biting the back of its neck or throat. Tigers can live for up to 26 years in the wild.

First draw circles for the head and for the front of the body.

Head

Draw an oval for the tiger's rear end.

Rear

Front body

Make a curved line for the tail.

Mark the eye position and the center of the face.

Back

Belly

Tail

Back legs

Front legs

Draw the curves of the back and the belly.

Add lines for the legs and indicate the ground they stand on.

Vital statistics

Human

Tiger

Tiger

Length

4.6—9.2 feet (1.4–2.8 m)

Weight

Up to 485 pounds (220 kg)

Draw in the ears.

Finish the shape of the tail.

Draw lines for the eyes and for the position of the nose and mouth.

Nose

Mouth

When drawing the legs and feet, imagine the tiger's body is a tube with legs set into it.

Draw the tiger's face and stripes.

Draw the stripes with a soft black pencil using marks that follow the fur's direction.

A tiger's orange and black stripes provide it with subtle camouflage in dappled light and shade.

15

Lion

The lion is the second largest of the big cats. Adult males can weigh more than 500 pounds (230 kg) and can measure more than 10 feet (3 m) long from tail to nose. A lion's roar can be heard up to 5 miles (8 km) away and is the loudest sound made by any big cat.

Draw circles for the head, muzzle, and rear and a large oval for the front of the body.

Rear

Head

Muzzle

Belly

Front

Draw lines under the belly and up to the muzzle.

Proportion

Use the size of the lion's head as a unit of measurement to help keep your drawing in proportion. The lion is 3 heads tall and its body is 3.5 heads long.

Mark out the eye line and the sides of the muzzle.

Back

Mane

Add lines for the position of the legs and the lion's feet. Draw lines for the back and tail.

Tail

Legs

Sketch in circles for the lion's mane and ears.

Draw a curved line to show the high arch of a lion's back.

Lightly draw in the shape of the eyes, nose and mouth.

Extend the line of the mane down to its belly.

Sketch in the front of the legs and the lion's paws.

Finish drawing the eyes, the nose and the mouth.

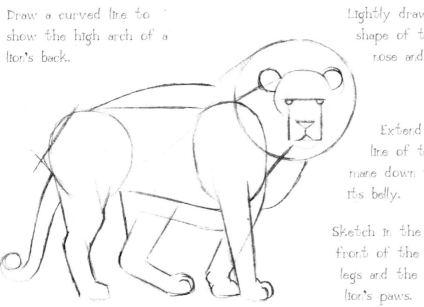

Make the lion's hindquarters more angular.

Draw the lion's mane using your pencil marks to follow the direction of the hair.

Finish drawing the hindquarters. Shade in the muscles.

A lion's mane can make a lion appear to be larger in size, which scares away other male lions.

17

Panther

A panther is a leopard or a jaguar with a black coat. Panthers are found in dense, dark tropical rain forests, where their coloring camouflages them well for hunting.

Chiaroscuro — Light and shade

When drawing a dark object, look to see which direction the light is coming from. Draw in the darkest parts of your subject first. Slowly build up the gray areas leaving some white paper showing through as the lightest parts of your drawing.

Draw circles for the head, front and rear of the body.

Back

Head

Rear

Belly

Front

Put in lines for the back and belly.

Tail

Sketch in a long curved tail.

Indicate the panther's eye position and draw a circle for its muzzle.

Neck

Eyes

Muzzle

Back legs

Draw in curved and straight lines for the back legs and feet.

Front legs

Add lines for its neck, front legs and feet.

18

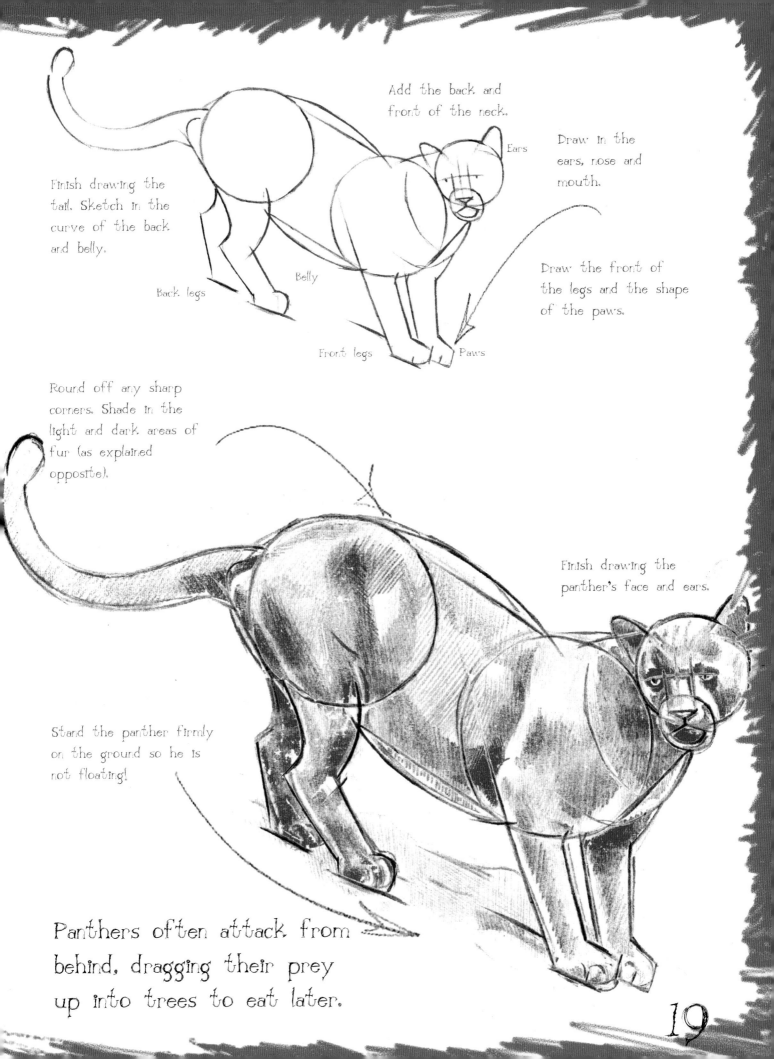

Add the back and
front of the neck.

Draw in the
ears, nose and
mouth.

Ears

Finish drawing the
tail. Sketch in the
curve of the back
and belly.

Back legs

Belly

Front legs

Paws

Draw the front of
the legs and the shape
of the paws.

Round off any sharp
corners. Shade in the
light and dark areas of
fur (as explained
opposite).

Finish drawing the
panther's face and ears.

Stand the panther firmly
on the ground so he is
not floating!

Panthers often attack from
behind, dragging their prey
up into trees to eat later.

19

Tiger's Head

An average male tiger stands 35 inches (90 cm) tall at shoulder height. Unlike other members of the cat family, tigers are not good tree climbers. However, they are strong swimmers and in floods, they are known to swim in search of stranded prey.

Eyes Highlight Shadow

Eyes are often the focal point of a drawing. Study and sketch the eyes of different animals. Look at the highlight on the eye and at the shape of the pupil.

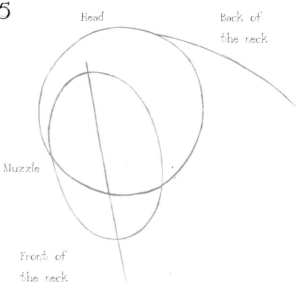

Draw a circle for the head and an oval for the muzzle.

Head

Back of the neck

Muzzle

Front of the neck

Add lines for the front and back of the neck.

Look carefully at the angle of the ears and draw them in. Indicate the eye position.

Ear

Ear

Upper Jaw

Lower Jaw

Draw two ovals, one for the lower jaw and the other for the upper jaw.

Draw two lines to join the lower jaw to the back of the mouth.

The maximum lifespan of a
tiger is usually around 26
years and for most of
their lives, tigers live alone.

Draw in the fur on
either side of its face.

Draw in the large
front teeth (top
and bottom).

Draw the tiger's
gums and the position
of its back teeth.

Draw the face and
eyes of the tiger.

Sketch in the
shape of the tiger's
stripes. Block in the
areas of gray tone first and
then the areas of dark tone.

Lastly, use a fine
paintbrush and white
paint for the paler
whiskers.

21

Leopard

Leopards are agile climbers and often haul their prey into the branches of a tree. They hunt alone and mainly at night. Each leopard has its own territory that it defends from other leopards.

Draw circles for the leopard's rear end, head and muzzle.

Rear

Head

Front leg

Muzzle

Sketch in the curve of the neck and back and the line of the front leg.

Draw the long curved line of the tail.

Tail

Back leg

Paw

Draw a circle for one ear and a triangle for the other.

Ears

Mark the position of the eyes and the muzzle.

Paw

Add straight lines for the back leg, and draw circles for the paws.

Make the leg shapes rounded to show the muscles in the legs and finish the paws.

Sketch in the neckline and the side of the face. Lightly draw in the eyes and nose. Add the lower jaw.

A leopard's spots make perfect camouflage in the dappled shade of a forest.

Lightly sketch in the leopard's markings.

Draw in the detail of the eyes, nose, ears and mouth.

Sketch in a tree branch. Look at the direction of light and put shadows under the leopard.

Finally, use white paint and a fine paintbrush to add the leopard's whiskers.

23

Lynx

Lynx are smaller than many other big cats. They live alone, mainly in pine forests, high up on mountain slopes. A lynx has a stubby tail, long tufted ears, a short body and large feet.

Draw circles for the head, front and rear ends of the lynx.

Front

Head

Rear

Construction lines

Study these drawings of a polar bear and a brown bear. Compare ear shapes. Check the position of their features. Using construction lines helps create three-dimensional looking drawings.

Sketch in the curve of the back and tail.

Back

Tail

Lightly mark a cross at the center of the head.

Put in straight lines for the back legs.

Back legs

Draw lines for the front legs and add circles for the paws.

Front legs

Paws

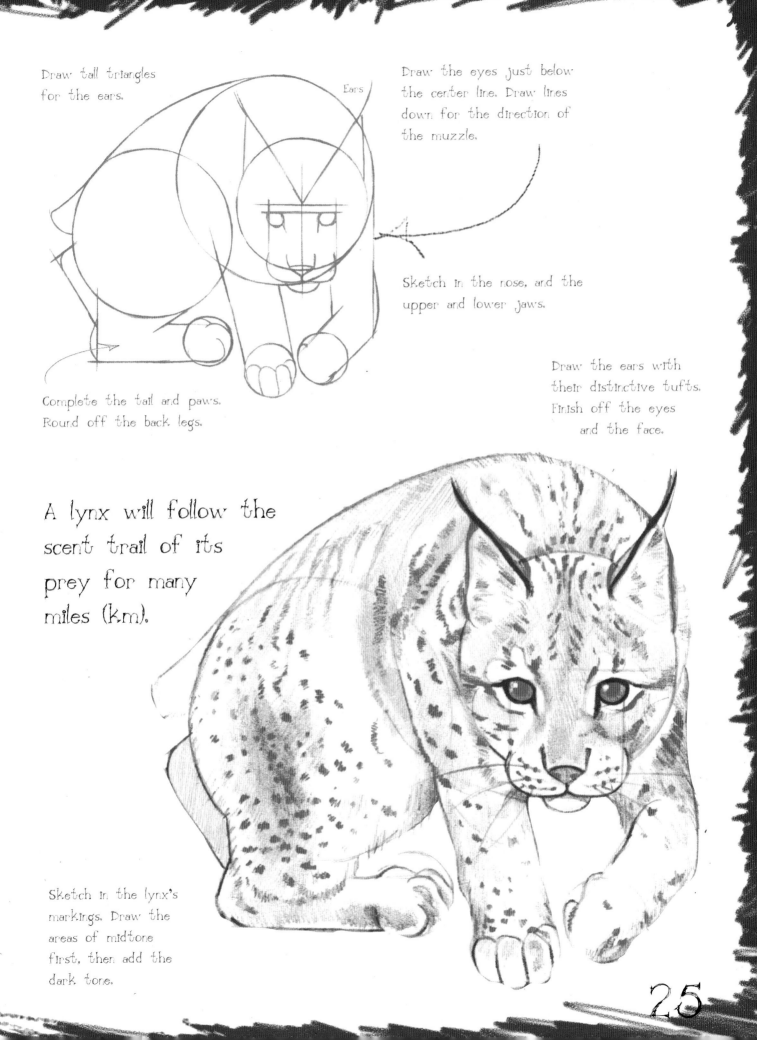

Draw tall triangles for the ears.

Ears

Draw the eyes just below the center line. Draw lines down for the direction of the muzzle.

Sketch in the nose, and the upper and lower jaws.

Complete the tail and paws. Round off the back legs.

Draw the ears with their distinctive tufts. Finish off the eyes and the face.

A lynx will follow the scent trail of its prey for many miles (km).

Sketch in the lynx's markings. Draw the areas of midtone first, then add the dark tone.

Cheetah

The cheetah is the world's fastest land animal. It can run up to 60 miles per hour (96 km/h). It hunts mainly in the early morning or twilight. Its preferred prey is either a Thompson's gazelle or an impala.

Draw circles for the head, front and rear end of the cheetah.

Add lines for its back and belly and indicate its neck.

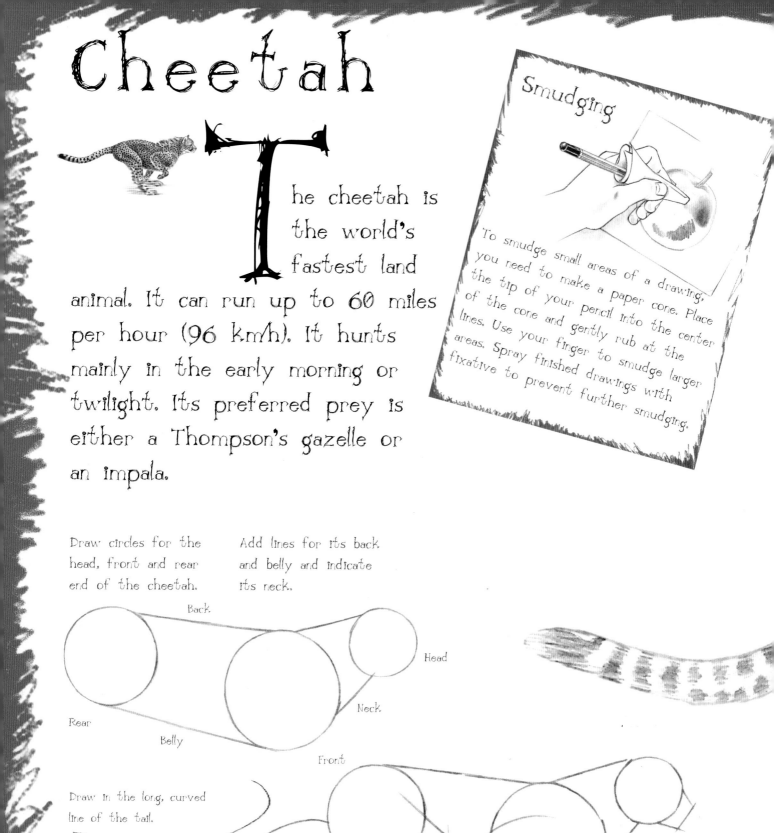

Back

Head

Neck

Rear

Belly

Front

Draw in the long, curved line of the tail.

Draw in the muzzle.

Draw in the lines for the legs. See how they make a triangular shape under the cheetah's body.

Finish the tail. It acts as a counterbalance to the rest of the cheetah's body.

Draw the ears and mane.

Curve the lines of the cheetah's back and belly.

Sketch in the eye, nose and mouth.

A cheetah has a streamlined body and a small head. Its long legs and flexible spine give the cheetah the maximum length of stride necessary for great speed.

Finish the legs and sketch in the paws. Round off all sharp angles.

Draw the cheetah's spotted coat. The tail markings begin as spots but gradually become stripes.

Draw in the face markings.

To give the impression of speed, carefully smudge both hind legs. (The drawing should still show through).

Lion Cubs

Lions live in family groups, called prides. Each pride consists of several females, their cubs and at least one male. Lion cubs start learning to hunt at about 11 months old but cannot catch prey until they are nearly 16 months old. A cub weighs about 3 pounds (1.3 kg) at birth and up to 507 pounds (230 kg) when adult.

Draw a circle for the head of the top cub and a line for its neck. Mark in its eye level.

Head

Neck

Head

Draw two circles for the head and body of the lower cub. Mark in its eye level.

Body of right cub

Ear

Draw circles for the ears and muzzles of both cubs.

Mark the position of their eyes.

Muzzle

Ear

Muzzle

Front legs

Draw in lines for their front legs and ovals for paws.

Composition

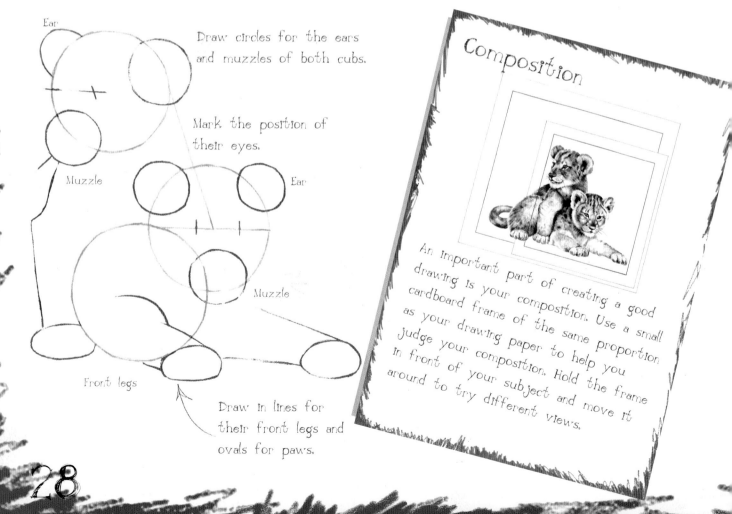

An important part of creating a good drawing is your composition. Use a small cardboard frame of the same proportion as your drawing paper to help you judge your composition. Hold the frame in front of your subject and move it around to try different views.

Study each cub's expression before drawing their eyes. Draw in each cub's nose and mouth.

Put dark tones on the faces.

Sketch in the ears. Finish drawing the paws and the front legs. Draw in the top cub's neck.

Puma

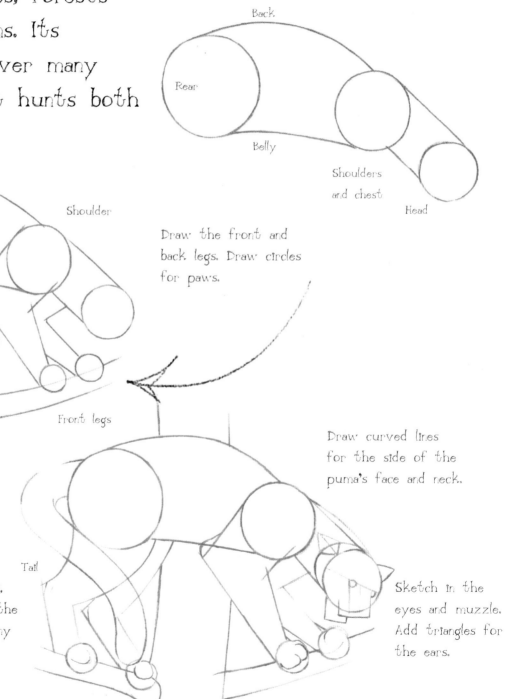

The puma is highly adaptable and makes its home in habitats as diverse as lowland prairies, forests or high mountains. Its territory can cover many miles (km) and it hunts both day and night.

Sketch in circles for the puma's head, chest, shoulders and rear end.

Draw curved lines for the back and belly. Draw the puma's neck.

Back

Rear

Belly

Shoulders and chest

Head

Draw the front and back legs. Draw circles for paws.

Shoulder

Tree trunk

Back legs

Front legs

Sketch the tree trunk and branches.

Draw curved lines for the side of the puma's face and neck.

Tail

Draw the puma's long, curved tail. Draw in the toes and round off any sharp angles.

Sketch in the eyes and muzzle. Add triangles for the ears.

A puma is a skillful jumper. From a standing position, it can leap onto a branch several feet (m) off the ground.

Checking your drawing

When you finish your initial sketch, hold it up to a mirror to check. The image will be in reverse and it will make any mistakes stand out.

Draw the puma's fur (notice that the fur on the tail is darker).

Block in the shadow cast on the tree by the puma.

Draw in the eyes, eye markings and ears.

31

Glossary

chiaroscuro (kee–AHR–uh–skyur–oh) The use of light and dark shades in a drawing or painting.

composition (kom–puh–ZIH–shun) The position of a picture on the drawing paper.

construction lines (kun–STRUK–shun LYNZ) Structural lines used in the early stages of a drawing.

fixative (FIK–suh–tiv) A type of resin used to spray over a finished drawing to prevent smudging. Fixatives should be used under adult supervision.

focal point (FOH–kul POYNT) A central point of interest.

light source (LYT SORS) The direction the light is coming from.

masking fluid (MAS–king FLOO–ud) A thin rubber solution, applied by brush to block off an area of a painting. It is peeled or rubbed off when dry.

proportion (pruh–POR–shun) The correct relationship of scale between parts of a drawing.

reference (REH–ferntc) Photographs or other images that can be drawn if drawing from life is not possible.

three–dimensional (three–deh–MENCH–nul) Having the effect of looking lifelike or real.

Index

B
ball–point pens 7

C
charcoal 4, 6, 12
cheetahs 26–27
chiaroscuro 18
composition 28
construction lines 24
crayons 4

F
felt–tip pens 5, 7, 13

fixative 6, 26
focal point 11, 20

I
ink 5, 7

L
leopards 9, 13, 22–23
lions 16–17, 28–29
lynx 24–25

M
mapping pens 7

marker pens 7
masking fluid 13

P
paint 4, 6, 13
paintbrushes 4, 7
panthers 18–19
paper 4, 6, 12–13
pastels 5–6, 13
pencils 4, 6, 13
photographs 10–11
proportion 16
pumas 30–31

S
shading, shadow 7, 11, 20
smudging 6, 26

T
three–dimensional (drawings) 11, 24
tigers 12–15, 20–21

W
watercolors 6, 12–13

Web Sites

Due to the changing nature of Internet links, PowerKids Press has developed an online list of Web sites related to the subject of this book. This site is updated regularly. Please use this link to access the list:

www.powerkidslinks.com/htd/bigcats/